Re
Reflections

Prayer-poems for Pocket or Pillow

Richard Whitfield

Bracken Bank Books

Resonant Reflections
Prayer-poems for Pocket or Pillow

Published in April 2006 by
Bracken Bank Books
Timber Hill, Lyme Regis
Dorset DT7 3HQ
United Kingdom

Telephone (UK): 01297-442529

ISBN 0-9538624-5-3
Printed and bound by
Creeds, Broadoak, Bridport, Dorset DT6 5NL

rw@richardwhitfield.co.uk

Also recently by Richard Whitfield:

Mastering E-Motions: *Feeling our Way Intelligently in Relationship*, O-Books, 2005

With Bruce Gilberd
(former Anglican Bishop of Auckland, New Zealand):

Taproots for Transformation:
*Nurturing Discernment and Leadership
in an Irrational World*
Shannon Press, Adelaide, 2006

Contents

Preface pages 4-6; Complementing books page 64

Poems on pages

Prayer-poems for Pocket or Pillow

Preface

We give power to that to which we give our attention. As reflective and sentient beings, we become the product of what we contemplate, think about, feel for, and dwell upon. Consequences of our inner, and often silent contemplations become manifest in both our demeanour and behaviour, whether this is crazy, crude, compassionate, creative, controlling, cramping or even crucifying.

In 1995 I was caught by surprise by a flood of poetic lines tumbling onto paper from my quiet contemplations. Later I sought advice about this surge from friends whose comments I could trust.

Robert Waldron, a lifetime teacher of High School English in Boston USA, whose highly perceptive and intelligible first book, *Thomas Merton in Search of His Soul: A Jungian Perspective* (Ave Maria Press, 1994), had impressed me, drew my attention to his short article

'*Poetry as Prayer*'. Then I had not the remotest thought that I might one day be impelled to compile a book of prayer-poems. I mused that even if some of my poetic lines might resonate with or even excite a few others, no way had I anything to offer that might be seen as prayer, a human activity over which, since childhood, I had felt a gregarious non-starter.

Religious literacy and affiliation do not guarantee, and may even impede spiritual development. A rather cosy, superficial belief system, immature for some of the challenges of mid-life, slowly became better distilled within me, aided by the poetic that I now know was hiding within me for most of a lifetime.

Presented here are further contours and colours of thought and feeling, gathered over the past four years, as a latent 'twin' to *Lifelines: Poems for Pocket or Pillow*. Launched at a *Gracenotes* recital within the biennial Meeting of the Thomas Merton Society, this book is dedicated to my young musician colleagues, Swedish soprano Karin Thyselius, and Zimbabwe pianist Michael Brownlee Walker .

The prayer-poems focus upon phases of human life, spiritual journeying and our endless challenge of learning to love life in ranges of reliable relationship. They invite slow ingestion as you 'shuffle into my shoes', polished for reflective purpose, and mirrored as short meditations. Aspects of these 'shoes' may fit where you now tread, whether in pain or pleasure, so resonating with your mind, mood and need, for we share similar soul longings. If at first some of phrases feel akin to paper aeroplanes flying over your head, with patience they may be seduced to land!

Prayer and contemplation do not demand prior belief, while head to head is dead without heart to heart. So may this poetry in motion be, for you, a love potion, shared as prayer.

Richard Whitfield
Lyme Regis, February 2006

Poet's Prayer

May I love words
Only for what they mean
When arranged on the page,
Punctuated by surprise
And an absence of lies.

May these words
Weave a shawl of serenity
Around your still growing child,
From centre to extremity.
May they
Ring around your sacred spaces,
Lift your sighs and singing,
With the cadent graces
Of liquid love
Flowing as warm hope, and healing
As you dance in moments of meaning
Upon your heart's home hearth.

Pockets and Pillows

In pockets perhaps
Hands, warmed, protective.
Tear-drying handkerchief
Clearing conduits of perception.
Money, exchange, change.
Keys to open up, or close down.
Spare buttons to hold togetherness.

Pillows upon bed await tired head
To comfort beyond toss and turn,
Sleep's, silence, dreams,
Illuminate the unconscious
Dark corners, screams,
Protecting, projecting, perverting,
Preventing pure Presence.

When and where placed,
From pocket or on pillow faced,
May these poems, as prayer,
Reflect in mind's eye
Your true hue and pliant sigh.

Pause Restores

Contemplation of nothing
But the empty silence
Slowly pulls us back, to track
The nature and substance of soul;
The good and pure original zest,
Early heartbeat's throbbing quest,
Unspoken hope and unformed prayer
Arriving in first breaths of air.

May we settle quietly away
From all matter, clutter, clatter,
And plans for the day
Masking our original gift condition,
Or infecting our blessed disposition;
Love sacramental, inside-out.
Is not a soul's sole purpose
The gift of love, and life devout?

As silence is transformed to song,
Calm contemplation reminds souls
Of where we best belong.

Society's First Law

Grave doubt
About our having the maturity
To avoid collapsing
In cascading emotional insecurity.

Society cannot hold as, in neglect
Of tender loving care,
Citizens' souls crumple, inward fold
Into an angry void of frozen cold
From childhood scar and scare.

So may we learn to live by love,
Prizing, enriching and enhancing
The beings and becomings
Of parents, partners,
Neighbours, family and friends,
Drowning indifference and hate,
Making amends
Before the nurture-dispossessed,
In disgust and deep distrust,
Storm the City's untended gate.

Do I Pray?

Amid a world
Of neglect, conflict, despair,
Do I have a single prayer,
Requiring listening,
Transforming deathly dross
To fine crystal, glistening?

Yes!
I pray for Peace;
For an end to all violence
To body, emotion,
Mind and soul.
Pray seeds of peace be sown
Within each heart
And in every home.

So may I become more alive
From inside-out,
As a pacemaker for peace.

Enlightenment

We need to know,
And much is known,
But in our acquisition and earning
We have lost
Languages of munificence
To express our deepest yearning
For spiritual significance.

In becoming more discerning,
May we cast off
Courageously
Upon the sea of solitude;
Prepared not to know,
Full of faith, faith at sea
Revoking fundamentalist formulae
Of spiritual immaturity
Breeding blinkered endearments
Yet false security,
To meet the real presence
Of mystery at the margins.

At those mandalic margins
Unknowing
Encounters enlightenment,
The silence of spheres,
The gift of lift,
And the promise of presence,
Passion, purpose,
As paradigm shift
Into the disarmed
Welcoming arms
Of Love's deep peace,
Our repressed condition
Locating lost language,
Re-bedding, renewing
Just life,
Trust life,
Time-warped belongings
Bound in ancestral tradition.

Well Connected

Each day
Let us pray
Of being well connected;
Of compassion come close
For lonely moments;
Of emotions gentling,
Minds protected,
Freed from fear
Through truths' clear fermenting.

Let us pray
For energies flowing in parallel;
For tasks resting lightly on lap;
For actions
Mindful, reflective,
Gaining good traction
Upon wounds and matters defective.

Then,
All manner of things
Will be well.

Everyday Graces

May Creation's majesty
    Empty my ego with awe;
    Fill my soul with wonder;
    Fuel my mind
    With wondrous questions;
    Heave my heart
    Towards respectful love;
    Move my e-motions
    Towards compassion;
    Bolster my breath
    With Holy Spirit.

Through these graces,
Shaping outer and inward man as one,
May I be used
As a faithful lover of life
At frontiers of daring
Divine conversation
At each intersection of life station.

Sense Meditation

Before eyes open,
Image great love;
Jesus in person,
Sighted.

Open ears to silence;
Hear Jesus as Word,
Fleshed as love;
Sounding.

Without haste,
Open buds to taste,
Fruits of field and vine,
Present in bread and wine;
Savouring.

Smell the fragrance of flowers;
Draw in fresh air,
Sing along to a Jesus song,
Lipped from soul to soul;
Scents of love inhaling.

Electromagnetism primes
Each heart beat,
Without pomp
As more than pump;
Miracle of blood and brain,
Sensing Spirit;
Love the power and purpose.
Take Jesus to heart's centre
As fine, freed universal mentor.

Reach out,
Touch his garment hem.
Open hands greet;
Meet
Jesus of the palms,
Love's fire at fingertips
Arc crib and cross.
Arms wait
Open wide,
At heart's gate;
Beckoning us to touch
Tentacles of Paradise.

Child Embrace

Our deepest longing
Is to be welcomed, cherished,
And to bloom
In each phased becoming
Through the tiny particulars
Of secure belonging.

Let our fervent prayer
Be to embrace all children
With best comfort care;
For tendered foundations
For good life,
Forming character, and constancy
Through joys, struggles and strife,
Nurtured long
In the uniqueness
And blessedness
Of each particular preciousness.

Peace Listening

Father and Mother in common,
Help us to listen
For the wisdom of peace,
Beyond bounds
Of culture and tradition.

May we hear the best words
Of playwright, poet and pastor,
The sharp memories of elders,
Stories of soldiers, sailors and sages
Down the ages
And the sacred dreams of children,
So perfecting pathways of love
Priming the lamp of peace.

Balance for Joy

Dearest One,
Help us
To sustain balance,
And equanimity
In encounter
With emotionally tender places,
Creating calm spaces
For reflection,
And correction of perception.

Threats to the soul
Are but a deception;
Beyond confusion and confinement
May they be our refinement,
Become gateways to joy
And contentment,
Graced, heaven sent.

Forgiving

To forgive is to liberate
The wounding Other,
Colleague, stranger, sister, brother,
From their weakness and failures,
And our Self from clamps
Of wounded disappointment.

To forgive is to vow brave acts,
For the greater good
Of refusing to repay
Wound with wound,
Evil with evil
On the anvil of life.

Dearest One,
Give us grace to forgive
Seventy times seven,
To make amends,
And to treat enemies and strangers
As if they are our friends.

Mutuality

Primed for mutuality,
We long to make perfect arches,
Keyed at confluences
Of nave and navel,
Holding, enfolding the head,
Heat and heart of matter,
Before we scatter from this Earth.

Mutuality is our saving grace,
For without another we have no face,
Or scope for faith and hope.

The human task,
When push comes to shove,
And without an ask,
Is delivery, beyond our birth,
Of gifts of reliable love.

So let us pray we may
Disdain all ego depravity,
Ever moved towards mutuality.

Dear Infant Voice

Listen to the Inner Voice
Of the tiny child,
Hidden as innocence inside
Clutching truth,
So strong, so pure, so mild.

Dear infant Voice divine,
Repressed, buried and dulled,
You remain life wine
Even when mauled
Or poorly mulled.

Still small infant Voice,
Pray return to my side,
Retune my frail spirit,
Drown my adult distractions
And superficial pride.

Turning

May melancholy
Be turned to hope,
Limitations
Given fresh scope;
Grief turned towards grandeur,
And anger calmed by candour.

May pain be transfigured
To good purpose and power,
And calm be present
At all times,
As tides go out, turn,
Come in,
And turn again,
Tight corners washed
At each upturning,
Limiting space extended
At each returning,
As cosmic mystery intended.

Wander Not

Pray:
No more wandering
Wondering
Of your beauty;
It is your duty
To enfold yourself
With compassionate love.

For Love made you,
And bade you
Welcome
In the house of the Universe;
And Love is forever there
As Imagination,
Its powers
Of tender touch
Contained safe within
Each long, longing
Silent prayer.

Aged Grace

May we grow old with grace,
Less distracted of form and face,
Wise around the eye,
Seeing beyond horizon, sky,
Exchanging limitation
For Christ-like imitation.

Pray
For the wisdom of perspective,
Reshaping roles
With less invective,
Opening empathy
More perceptive
Of aches and wounds of souls,
Ever holy,
And,
With love's soft, patient touch
Growing into greater wholes.

Open Face

In life's thick and thrall,
Pray we pay our dues
To the many hues
Of taking bat to ball,
Splicing and spicing
Our lives with stillness,
Beyond the illness
Of hyperactivity,
Losing design and shape,
Filling every void and cavity
With time-warped escape.

May we seek and recover
A slower life pace
So as to be life
With an open face,
Become an aqueduct for grace.

Evening Prayer

Great Sustainer:
    Who brings in the days,
    Who rejoices amid gladness,
    Who cries amid sadness,
    Who gives life flavour,
    Rich foods to savour;
    Who, listening,
    And hearing all,
    Gives all both hope and voice,
    So many reasons to rejoice.

Be near us this night,
Comfort our spirits,
Protect our sleep from harsh dreams
In darkness sowing fears of loss;
Show us the beauty that redeems,
Make purpose of our aimless dross.
By seeing all, give all a face;
And life abundant fused in grace.

Magnanimity

May we move to magnanimity;
Enfold Earth's majestic variety;
Know the soils and rocks;
Learn from sand and sea;
Walk towards the light.

May we keep open eyes,
Kiss the rinse of tears,
Reach for open skies,
Conquer all destructive fears.

May we be watchful
Of ebbs and flows of relationship
Beyond skin deep,
The hidden tenderness of nurture
Never fast asleep.

Magnanimity
Embroidered, emboldened,
Imprinted beyond our days,
Brave recognitions and responses
Reflect our highest praise.

War and Peace

We are a species of conflict,
Whether with, without, or within;
Lack of considerate love the sin
From the cradle to the grave;
Yet love bequeaths power to save.

Peace is our deepest desire
As wars waste
At home, in homes, and away;
Warring foremost an attitude
Of ingratitude,
As strife shrinks, shames life;
And each war wound,
No less than each love song,
Cascades consequences.

Holding my conflicts in check,
I pray that I may
Make peace today,
First inside,
Then out, far and wide.

Beyond Vanity

Much is power and vanity,
Overactive ego,
Compassionless insanity,
And preventable human calamity.

Powers we allow
Design
Spun sugared half truths
For our time,
Coloured candy floss,
Unwholesome gloss,
Remote from secure lifeline,
Lightweight without light,
Consuming images dead as dross.

May we be brave and bold;
Change the range
Of our presumptions,
Creating summer sanctuaries
To house our dreams.

Reframing

False mind frames deceive,
And we creatures
Scarcely perceive
Our marking with divine features.

May we
    Deepen our discernment;
    Plumb our imagination
    Protect our first purity;
    Open casement to candour,
    To amazement and to grandeur.

And may we move
    From error to truth,
    From indifference to love,
    From despair to hope,
    From darkness to light,
    From fear to friendship,
    And from pain to gain.
Again, and again and again.

An Overcoming

Waves of words,
Seeming new,
Yet far from few
Amidst
The mist
Of clouded eye,
Teardrops' dew
A muffled cry,
Now repeat
Tide and times,
Tap and beat
Of inner air,
Shorter lines,
Silent prayer.

May our days
Take care
In motion,
Melt as praise
With Love's devotion.

Confident to Love

Love is not material mass
Slipping through our fingers,
But a grace and blessing
Of giving fine Spirit
Already recognised and received.

Love cannot be imposed,
Only evoked,
Demonstrated, tendered,
Stroked,
Provoked
Within each being,
As refreshed becoming.

So let us pray
For courage and confidence to love,
Strength for the journey of love;
Dignity through the pain of love;
And for gratitude and awe
Amid the power and peace of love.

Adolescent Energy

May each adolescence
Be full of effervescence
Great idealism,
Great visions,
Great expectations,
Unabashed,
Never dashed.

May each adult child
In midlife storm or stall,
When regeneration is the call,
Recall
Fine energies of youth
To search afresh
For tone and truth.

Magical Me?

May love's inner discipline
Channel me
To hold you
With respect
As wholly Other,
Not some mythic, magical sister,
Brother, spouse, friend or lover
Bound to fall below my expectations.

Then I may discover
My magical inner Self;
Become more magical in being,
Blooming in gardens of Eden,
Become more magical in seeing,
Glimpsing paradise found,
Rooted in holy ground
Where the tuneful true Other
May be heard and found
Within the innocence of infancy.

Pride and Process

Full of fine intention,
Once proud as an action man,
My commitment and convention
Being ever busy, forming and fixing.
So I ran, and I ran, and I ran,
Making marks on sands of time,
Plans, meetings, budgets,
Letters, 'phones and fax.
The crime of many a busy bee
Too ready to sting,
No time to relax,
No time to sing.

So let us pray
For the sway of energies
To permit our innermost
To be of slow, leisurely flow
Far wiser than a driven self,
One fine-tuned
To the hidden in Creation
And our common wealth.

Mirror Wise

Mingling
Among the wide open
Beauties and bounties
Of Nature,
I dare brief glances
In the mirror
Of my own true nature

To stop, stand and stare
Into my own deep
Nature's eyes,
Horizons for longing,
Belonging,
Framing call and cry
Of land, sea and sky,
Is just this prayer,
For just one day;

Pray, let it be today!

Good Fortune

May we dive deep
Into the warm waters
Of innerness.
Swim naked
Amongst the passions
Of words
As they penetrate
Presence and purpose,
Allowing the tropical fish
To tickle our toes
With tenderness
Before we resurface
To catch our breath,
Buoyed by the upward
Thrust of lotus love
For fresh flowerings
Of faith in action.

Fitting?

Not always in the right place
At the right time,
May we learn
From where we do not fit.

To find a right
From within each wrong place
Is no disgrace
As we grapple in darkness
With conscience and call,
Until finding light of face
Before the dread of our final fall.

Along each pockmarked journey,
Lies a welcome rest,
A serving place,
Cleared, and shining
Within an orb of grace.

Locked Love

Pray that we may
Be wide open,
So disown
The double wound,
The double ache
Of too much love locked in,
Less give,
And
Too much love locked out,
Less gain;
For both go against the grain
Of natural companionship.

Reconnecting

Feel each tainted,
Tangled, tinted tingle
As you mingle
Underground,
Over ground,
With the sorrows of your soul.

Resolve to let those rest.
Stretch your scenery,
Expand your chastened chest;
Review your greenery
In full summer's best.
Pick up afresh,
Lift
Life's free gift,
Reconnected
To your bliss
And zest.

Shamed Spirit

Soul-spirits are original blessings.
Social projection
Into shamed dejection
Is neither account nor reflection
Of others' wound and imperfection.

God knows we struggle inside
With social shame,
A learned bad habit,
More than we dare admit.
This long shadow keeps us locked
Inside ourselves, away from others
In the same leaky, lonely boat,
Wrestling, separated, to stay afloat.

So let us pray that we may discard
The shackles of shabby shame;
Melt our embarrassments
By shuffling closer to candlelight,
Deepening our relating and mating,
Freeing passion and compassion.

Always Christmas

The Incarnation mystery
Is divinely human history
In all times and places,
Word birthed, mystery
Speaking to our vacant spaces.

Christmas
Is a time of modest stable welcome,
Of a child, just like you and I;
A birthing anniversary with presents.

He gave of a selfless Love.
Each Christmas birthday
What are our Happy Returns to Him?

Silently, patiently, he beckons
Our male and female hearts;
Enquires of our hopes and hurts,
Longs for our active devotions
Transcending time,
His love work, unfinished,
Need undiminished.

In prayer, amid our busyness,
Let us offer for transformation
All our business,
Finished and unfinished,
So that wheat, chaff and tares
May reflect a truer likeness,
Our infant mirrored in His infancy.

From our silent reflections,
Joys and dejections,
Let us perpetuate His teaching,
His giving, His passion,
Handing on the baton
Of His grace, healing
Care and compassion,
Serving with songs of serenity.

For God is patient, Love Divine,
Present far less in creeds
Than in everyday ways of mingling,
Present in every caring, sharing,
Symbolised in bread and wine.

Greened Sage

Amid stubborn downdrafts,
May we recall
Sacred breath
As warm wind
Beneath wings
Frozen of feeling.

Sense signs,
Siftings,
Shifting,
Uplifting,
Softening shadowing
Contours and colours
Of sense and soul.

See sure silvered
Greened sage,
Called by Page;
Pray developing,
Ever growing
As we age.

Oceans of Oxygen

May we take deep breaths
As we dive deep
Into image,
Imagination,
Dream and destiny;
Prospecting spiritual mysteries
Beyond the linear logic
Of our crimped consciousness.

May we feel the space
Of the ocean surge,
Yielding oxygen for the soul
Amid rip tides
And tender tidings,
Before resurfacing,
Regenerated by surprise,
Without doubting
Our blessedness.

Come Composure

As we sit,
Silently waiting;
Lost among wound and word,
May our composing
Find enough composure
Before disclosure
Of shape from shard.

Spits, spats and sparks
Prompt rifts,
Splits,
Rafts,
Even Noah's arks.

As life is shared
Or pinched and spared
In common,
Witness tokens
Of the joined
And the broken.

Moral Moves

Arising from the disposition
Of acquisition
Of stuff and status,
Let us move
Through labyrinths of loss:

> From control to contentment,
> From mourning to meaning,
> From lust to love,
> From purgatory to presence,
> From whining to wisdom,
> And through grief to growth.

Such moral moves
Of rebirth and regeneration,
Transcendence and transformation,
Are shape and substance
For every soul's salvation.

Target Mania

With neither purpose,
Nor well measured aim
We should feel some shame,
And take the blame
For our blinkered blindness
Of neglect of good service,
Reflecting trust, truth
And loving kindness.

May public servants:
Educators, social and health carers,
Priests and policy sharers
Be spared from losing the point
Of fine moments of focus,
Through misplaced target mania,
And adjunct paper paraphernalia,
The thrust of pervasive distrust,
Accounting lost to breath,
Auguring civic and spiritual death.

Depress, Confess

For humankind, born as body, spirit,
Mind, yet emotionally blind,
Storms of murk,
Lurk in hidden corners of life;
And under carpet or counter
May await strife.

Black clouds, dark woods,
Dank waters, foggy dreams depress
Inner screams for flowing streams
Of love and laughter.
Such underground alchemies press
Spiritual transformation from distress.

Lord, melt our protective hardness
So that liquid love
Can flow through our veins,
For we must be born-agains;
Winged angelic children of light,
Ends burning, turning
New beginnings into bright delight.

Healing Feeling

Some of us are models of efficiency,
Too busy to think
Of what we are feeling.
Others, sorely unproductive, drowsy,
Are deadened,
Under the weight of feeling lousy.
Yet others oscillate
Between these poles,
Bravely searching for their souls.

Reflecting on human form and feeling
Prompts questions, to set us reeling
About unconscious voices
Silently censoring our concepts,
Images and choices.

So we pray for moderation
Of action, and reaction
To all narrows, slings and arrows;
Thence deep healing
Of bad feeling.

Madonna

Precocious, pouting
Precious Pop Star,
I feel from afar
The jump and joy
Of your sad and angry energy.

May this shame
All destructive game
And pernicious gain,
Shining fresh light afar,
In every boudoir
And corridor of power
Where Love's promise
Is not premise.

For the tiny but far from puny me,
I pray to hold and see
Myself as an energetic point of light,
Linked to others' deep truths aright,
Together an incandescent sight,
Locked as One Love.

To Tranquillity
(Thanks to Australian cartoonist, Michael Leunig)

Let me keep a stock of new brooms
For clearing my floor
And door of clutter.

Then I may lay down
The rug of constancy
And relax
In the armchair of reflection.

Taking a good book, speaking of life.
I soak in fine words and thoughts,
Draining the teapot of truth
Into the cup of faith and hope.

I pause to be graced by true love,
Actively seeded at the start,
So that I may flower more freely
In the vase of Divine Tranquillity,
Glowing on the mantelpiece,
Priceless peace.

Open Up

Before we can live love
We must truly love love;
Image love, dwell on love,
Permit love, breathe love,
Fall in love with love,
Choose to love moment by moment,
To be and become beloved
Beyond banal boundaries.

If love is let out
Love is let in.
This is the only command;
To decline the only sin;
For to dwell
Shut out, shut in, without Love,
Is emotional and spiritual hell.

May we dare open up
Inside-out to Love's welcome,
So drink from the bottomless cup
Of kindness.

Self Portraits

Do we pine, or shine
At the shrine of providence?

On the touchlines of life
We tend to pout and shout,
Or shrink into dark pink
On the brink of being.

May we discover wisdom
In ruthless gaze upon life, phased,
Stretched between the pivot points
Of birth and death,
Brain, bond, breakage and breath.

Looking life in the eye
Is the soul's constant pleasure,
Constant cry.
So, by the day we die,
May we all create
A secret centred, scented
Self-portrait,
Good enough to love.

Eternal Lullaby

Come dear Love
And sit with neighbour and me
Under a plain and simple tree
Bearing all messages of time;
Roots unseen,
Leaves to shelter,
Beyond all helter-skelter,
And sing an eternal lullaby
So we may cry with joy,
Despite an aching universe,
Diverse,
Often perverse,
But for the love You sing
And the love we bring,
Sharing our care,
Our worship
And our prayer.

Hide and Seek

God hides
In many forms,
Beyond the dark,
Beyond our storms
And anguish, stark;
But, most of all, lost within
Our sorrows,
Gnawing at our sin,
Moving through the bile,
Matters vile,
Through pains
Veins, blood,
Despond,
Seeing beyond
The clog of fog and mud.

Knowing all our foolish errors,
Trials, tribulations, terrors,
Subtly God presents
Compassion, friendship, effervescent.

How can we resent
This hidden form revealed,
In Creation, present
In particulars of incarnation,
Image, and imagination?

Let us pray
We will respond
To Being,
Simply bidden
To seek the hidden
In living fronds,
Immanent and beyond.

Know the Trinity of Loves:
The One,
Earthly Mother with Son,
And Holy Spirit,
Free for everyone.

So resolve to seek, espy
Unconditional loves
With a spry third eye,
Grace-winged by angels and doves.

Open Wide

May we be open wide vessels
With only parasols
To shield extremes of climate.

May we be ever ready
For friendship,
And fresh air,
Breaks and breath for prayer.

Sailing beyond horizon,
Sometimes tossed
Over long days,
May we never lonely,
Never lost
Of wonder, love and praise.

Best

May best words
Be taken to heart,
Kept in mind,
Mirrored in intentions
And actions,
With patient love
In all transactions.

Revolving
(Acknowledging closing lines of Dante's Divine Comedy)

May we be daily renewed,
Reliable as a wheel that spins
With even motion,
Revolved by the Love
Moving planets and stars.

Injunctions

Pray we may
Scuff away
The froth and flotsam
Of shoreline
Before we decay
And decline.

May we love the light,
Whatever the source.
Love our life,
Through every stage
Of its winding, surprising course.
Love the rose,
Whatever the scent or soil,
Seeking and living
Our truth,
Whatever the toil.

Ripened Days

Time strips each kingdom bare
Of wheat and tare;
Each tiny earth world tended
Finally denuded
Of our particular fare and care.

May each dawning day
Of gift life
Be experienced
As wide-ranging readiness,
And ripeness.

May our loves
Be not disabled by sadness,
But fortified by awareness;
And death,
Accepted gently
When it comes,
Just as each newborn life
Emerges that same hour,
Hovering with hope.

Complementing Books

Lifelines: Poems for Pocket or Pillow
Richard Whitfield
64 pages, 2004, ISBN 0 9538624 4 5   £2.50

Three books of poetic commentary on life:

Transformations: A Spiritual Memoir
Richard Whitfield
80 A5 pages, 2000, ISBN 0 9538624 0 2   £6.00

Purpose in Presence:
Cameos on Attachment and Social Action,
Richard Whitfield
80 A5 pages, 2001, ISBN 0 9538624 1 0   £6.00

Messages in Time: Life Path, Love's Pattern
Richard Whitfield
80 A5 pages, 2002, ISBN 0 9538624 2 9   £6.00

****

Paintings with complementing poems:
Mindscapes of Meaning: Paging the Soul
Eva Maria Barry and Richard Whitfield
ISBN 0-9538624-3-7
64 pages, 2003, with 30 full colour plates £8.50

****

Please add £1 for postage for single book orders.

Bracken Bank Books

Timber Hill, Lyme Regis, Dorset, DT7 3HQ
Telephone (UK): 01297-442529